THE
U.S. CONSTITUTION
FOR EVERYONE

Produced and Illustrated by
MORT GERBERG

A Perigee Book

Special Thanks to . . .

James MacGregor Burns, Woodrow Wilson Professor of Political Science, Emeritus, Williams College; Leonard W. Levy, Andrew W. Mellon All-Claremont Professor of Humanities and Chairman, Graduate Faculty of History, Claremont Graduate School, and Editor in Chief, *Encyclopedia of the American Constitution*; James H. Hutson, Chief, Manuscript Division, Library of Congress; Milton Cantor, Professor of Constitutional History, University of Massachusetts, Amherst; Dr. Bernard A. Weisberger; Richard B. Bernstein, Research Curator of The New York Public Library's Constitution Bicentennial Project; Project '87—the American Historical Association and the American Political Science Association for the American Constitutional Bicentennial; Robert Lewis Shayon, Professor of Communications, The Annenberg School of Communications, University of Pennsylvania, and creator of *You Are There;* Pauline Maier, Professor of History, and Head, History Faculty, Massachusetts Institute of Technology; Dianne Francesconi Lyon, National Archives Volunteer, Secretary Constitution Study Group; The Ford Foundation, for *The Constitution,* by Joseph N. Welch, with Richard Hofstadter and The Staff of *Omnibus.*

And Very Special Thanks to . . .

Jerome Agel, the polymath whose formidable constitution has made of this book a more Perfect Union.

Perigee Books
are published by
The Putnam Publishing Group
200 Madison Avenue
New York, NY 10016

The author gratefully acknowledges The Ford Foundation for permission to reprint a section of
The Constitution as edited by Joseph N. Welch.

Library of Congress Cataloging-in-Publication Data

United States.
    The U.S. Constitution for everyone.

    "A Perigee book."
    Summary: Presents the text of the Constitution,
explains its fundamentals, and traces events
leading up to its adoption in 1788.
    1. United States—Constitution.
2. United States—Constitutional
law. [1. United States—
Constitution. 2. United States—Constitutional
law] I. Gerberg, Mort. II. Title.
    KF4527.U55   1987   342.73'02   86-30322
    ISBN 0-399-51305-1   347.3022

Cover design Copyright © 1987 by Joshua Max

Typeset by Fisher Composition, Inc.

Printed in the United States of America

17

In the course of human events, in the 1780s, "We the People" of the nascent United States of America—white, male, principally Protestant, and mostly motivated (some say) by pocketbook patriotism—came to feel keenly that the instrument of government framed by the "traitorous" Founding Fathers during the stress of the eight-year Revolutionary War against the English wasn't working. "The firm league of friendship" that was to be the "perpetual Union" of the 13 former colonies was, in the words of the revered George Washington, "always moving upon crutches and tottering at every step," a crippled ship of state floundering at home and all but ignored abroad. "Without some alteration in our political creed," Washington warned, "the superstructure we have been . . . raising at the expense of so much blood and treasure must fall: we are fast verging to anarchy and confusion."

Under the radical-inspired Articles of Confederation drafted a few days after the Declaration of Independence, the President was merely a figurehead (the one-house Confederation Congress' presiding officer, with no independent status or power), and the Congress (one vote per state) was impotent. It was only a "diplomatic assembly" with a fundless treasury and no power to tax, regulate commerce, keep the peace at home, oust the British from outposts on the northern frontier, force Spain to let Americans sail on the lower Mississippi, or liberate American seamen held hostage by Mediterranean corsairs.

The central government was in fact subordinate to the 13 "Disunited States of America"—13 separate, sovereign, selfish rivals feuding sectionally and commercially and "all tugging at the Federal head." Nine of the states had their own navies. Seven printed non-interchangeable paper-money issues, and several imposed trade tariffs on neighboring states and unjust laws on their own citizens. Some disregarded private property beyond their own borders and some flung lead at newcomers—Pennsylvania troops near Wilkes-Barre, for instance, blasted away at settlers from Connecticut. And New Jersey, jarred by the postwar depression and suffocated by New York impost policies, lurched on the brink of either dissolution or a merger with New York or Pennsylvania.

Some of the citizenry *were* satisfied with the way things were going. Government wasn't on their backs. It wasn't trespassing on their liberties. But "the better sort" had had enough of the "embarrassing" tumult. They were powerful, celebrated, and articulate—and they had clout. For them, the American Revolution wasn't over. The nation *needed* a strong central government with authority to help carry out the public business. And so when intellectual, political, and generational events came together, the superpatriots (some say heroically, some say lawlessly) moved to form that "more Perfect Union . . . to secure the Blessings of Liberty to ourselves and our Posterity." Through the long, hot summer of 1787, they composed "a miracle"— the *Constitution of the United States.* It was inherently ambiguous. It was, in Alexander Hamilton's phrase, "a bundle of compromises," paradoxically entrenching both liberty and slavery. But its fundamental principles and laws and its new institutions are still transforming the nation, making us (in Washington's immortal words) "the happiest people upon Earth."

Rural insurrections had finally triggered the great "experiment." In mid-1786, "a black cloud rose in the east and spread over the west" when debtor farmers took up stave and pitchfork against foreclosures and jail sentences. It was another "shot heard 'round the world." Terrified landowners, merchants, and bankers demanded *action*: uprisings such as Shays's Rebellion in Massachusetts *had* to be curbed, the states unified, order maintained. "Let us have [a government] by which our lives and liberties and properties will be served," Washington insisted, "or let us know the worst at once." At an Annapolis conference of five states, James Madison, convinced that "most of our political evils may be traced to our commercial ones," and Hamilton, the cocksure "bastard son of a Scotch pedlar," masterminded a resolution asking all 13 states to send representatives to a conclave in Philadelphia the following May (1787) to "take into consideration the trade and commerce of the United States" and to address all issues necessary "to render the Constitution of the Federal government adequate to the exigencies of the Union."

In New York, the Confederation Congress, powerless to deal with agrarian revolts and the deterioration of state governments, cautiously gave legal status to the Annapolis proposal by setting a "grand convention" in centrally located,* crime-ridden, insufferably muggy, Quakerish Philadelphia *"for the sole and express purpose of revising the Articles of Confederation* and reporting to Congress and the several legislatures such alterations and provisions therein."

Only one state, Rhode-Island and Providence Plantations, refused to attend. Its rural "leaden-headed legislators"—*Rogue Islanders*—wanted no interference with their popular cheap-money schemes which other states viewed as the scourge of sound credit, reason enough for Connecticut and Massachusetts conservatives to want to strike the littlest state out of the Union and divide the territory between its neighbors.

The legislatures of the 12 other states named 74 delegates in total. Eventually, 55, half of them lawyers, showed up. Eight had signed the Declaration of Independence 11 years earlier. John Dickinson had refused to be a signator, but he then drafted the basis for the Articles of Confederation; now he was very much for a new charter if the rights of the small states weren't trampled. Presently, 13 of the 55 delegates

---

*The infant republic, at least three-quarters agricultural, was huge and travel was difficult. Georgia alone was larger than the whole of England. Boston (population 18,000) to New York (33,000) by stagecoach took a week. Most people lived within 100 miles or so of the Atlantic Ocean.

quit: nine for personal reasons, four for ideological reasons. (Maryland's irascible, brandy-belting Luther Martin went home to use his tigerish lawyer skills to try to deflect ratification of the "conspiracy"'s "total abolition and destruction of all state governments.") There was an average daily attendance of 30. It's been called a convention of "the well-bred, the well-fed, the well-read, and the well-wed." ·

Several celebrated Americans *weren't* on hand. The magnetic, volcanic advocate of states' rights, Patrick Henry, self-appointed "sentinel" over the liberty and happiness of all Virginians, "smelt a rat"; the erstwhile governor's "disgust exceeded all measure," and he stayed away. The forceful political theorist John Adams and unity-oriented Thomas Jefferson were representing the U.S. abroad. The aging firebrand Samuel Adams and Paul Revere and Governor John Hancock had not been named to the Massachusetts delegation. John Jay was busy in New York as Congress' shrewd Secretary for Foreign Affairs, and Aaron Burr didn't seem to be interested.

No women were on hand, either; they had no political rights, and suffered an inferior legal position. There were no blacks; 40 percent of the Southern population was in bondage—the way West was to be "paved with Negroes." And there were no Native Americans; Indian tribes, waging guerrilla wars almost everywhere, were seen as foreign nations with which treaties would have to be negotiated. (The Confederation Congress had sent to the Cherokee an offer tantamount to statehood.)

The convention would have been doomed without George Washington's participation. He was like Joshua of old. He commanded the sun and the moon to stand still, and they did. Washington had commanded the pick-up Continental Army to victory over the Redcoats, and he was the most popular man in the country. After wavering on attending, he rode into Philadelphia to the pealing of the Liberty Bell and was unanimously chosen to be the presiding officer. "To see this country happy," he said, "is so much the wish of my soul." Washington spoke only once during the convention—on the very last day. He dominated the proceedings with royal mien and severe dignity, his gray eyes and frown (and smile) revealing his sentiments.

The second most celebrated delegate was also the oldest: Benjamin Franklin. At 81, the fat, squat lightning-tamer and president of Pennsylvania was so stricken with gout he had to be carried to Independence Hall in a sedan chair on the shoulders of convicts.

"The father of the Constitution," a title he renounced, emphasizing always that the charter was a collective work, was James Madison, indefatigable despite a weak constitution. His 15-resolution Virginia Plan generated the disregard of Congress' mandate, the scrapping of the feckless Articles, and the throttling of parochial power struggles. Madison proposed a legislature of two houses representing the states proportionally, plus a National Executive and a national judiciary chosen by the legislature. An enlarged sphere of government would dilute the power and passion of local factions—"a strong consolidated. Union in which the idea of states should be nearly annihilated." It was the "rat" Patrick Henry had smelt.

The question of equal versus proportional representation in the legislature became the focus of harsh debate. How would the smaller states defend themselves against the giants (Virginia, Pennsylvania, Massachusetts)? Should the slaves be counted as whole people (giving the South a lock on control)? The four-month "assembly of demigods"—Jefferson's description—struggled in almost total secrecy. "Sentries are planted without and within—to prevent any person from approaching near . . ." The crusty states' rights advocate George Mason noted, "This I think myself a proper precaution to prevent mistakes and misrepresentations until the business shall have been completed, when the whole may have very different complexion from that in which the several crude and undigested parts might in their first shape appear if submitted to the public eye."

Delegates battled over the relationship between government and the people, how the powers of the three-branched government should be deployed, and whether the North should press for abolition and face a Southern walkout and probable collapse of the convention. At times, dissolution was only "a hairsbreadth away."

In mid-July, Roger Sherman, unwigged, cunning, self-educated, a Yankee-drawled Calvinist, was the major architect of the thrice-proposed Connecticut Compromise that finally broke the deadlock on representation: There should be proportional power for the states in the lower chamber, the House of Representatives (the total of white residents plus three-fifths of black, a carryover from the Confederation), and equality in the upper chamber, the Senate.

An intellectual breakthrough made possible the contrivance of an acceptable Federal system. Sovereignty lay not in government (and hence not in the governments of the individual states) but in the people themselves. *The people* were the source of all power. Because the Second Continental Congress (1775) existed *before* the states, James Wilson (Pa.) said, the American nation thus came first; the states could not legitimately claim to have created the federal government. Because sovereignty resided in the people, the state governments could never lose sovereignty they had never had. *The governors were the servants of the governed.*

Then uniquely, "We the People" gave power to the government they had created, incorporating the promise of democracy into political institutions. In a decision that has come to define the very character of the American political system, power would be divided and fragmented through a system of checks and balances designed to maintain the rigid balance between order and liberty. ("The different governments will control each other at the same time that each will be controlled by itself," Madison forecast.) The strong central government would be supreme in certain areas. Rights would be reserved to the states and to the people. There would be respect for law, order, and property rights. The building of a great, commercially powerful nation was indeed possible. The South received the national sanction of slavery—several clauses were "a monument to Southern craft and gall"—and the North was able to tie taxation to representation.

The "miracle at Philadelphia"—that "bundle of compromises"—the mortar binding the 50-state edifice under the concept of federalism, safeguarding our liberties and simultaneously energizing and restraining the nation—survives. At all times and under all circumstances, those four pages of prescient parchment (and 26 amendments) still protect all 241,000,000 of us in our beliefs, our thoughts, our emotions, and our sensations.

Happy birthday! Happy birthday to *us*!

THE CONSTITUTION
OF THE UNITED STATES OF AMERICA

Ratified in 1788

PREAMBLE

We the People of the United States, in order to form a more perfect union, establish justice, insure domestic tranquillity, provide for the common defense, promote the general welfare, and secure the blessings of liberty to ourselves and our posterity, do ordain and establish this Constitution for the United States of America.

Article 1

LEGISLATIVE DEPARTMENT

Section 1. **Congress in General**

All legislative powers herein granted shall be vested in a Congress of the United States, which shall consist of a Senate and a House of Representatives.

Section 2. **The House of Representatives**

a. Election and term of members. The House of Representatives shall be composed of members chosen every second year by the people of the several States, and the electors in each state shall have the qualifications requisite for electors of the most numerous branch of the State Legislature.

b. Qualifications of members. No person shall be a Representative who shall not have attained to the age of twenty-five years, and been seven years a citizen of the United States, and who shall not, when elected, be an inhabitant of that State in which he shall be chosen.

c. Apportionment of representatives and of direct taxes. Representatives and direct taxes shall be apportioned among the several States which may be included within this Union, according to their respective numbers, which shall be determined by adding to the whole number of free persons, including those bound to service for a term of years, and excluding Indians not taxed, three-fifths of all other persons. The actual enumeration

(All-capital and bold face headwords, such as LEGISLATIVE DEPARTMENT and **Congress in General** above, have been added as reader guides. Underlined material in the Constitution is no longer applicable.)

The oldest written constitution in the world, notes Professor Judith A. Best, created a democratic Federal republic: "We are not, never have been, and were not intended to be a simple democracy, because a simple democracy is a form of tyranny—a majority tyranny."

About 3,000,000 whites and 50,000 free blacks. (In 1845, John Louis O'Sullivan, justifying the annexation of Texas, wrote in the *Democratic Review,* "Our manifest destiny is to overspread the continent allotted by Providence for the free development of our yearly multiplying millions.")

The 52-word Preamble grants no power to the Federal government but helps in the interpretation of the Constitution.

Delegate Elbridge Gerry (Mass.) argued that annual elections were "the only defense of the people against tyranny."

Women were never explicitly denied office. But not until 1917 did Republican Jeannette Rankin (Mont.) become the first woman to sit in the House, three years before women won the right to vote for President.

Changed by Section 2 of the 14th Amendment.

"Slavery! That peculiar institution! That firebell in the night!" (Free blacks had the rights of citizenship.)

A euphemism for slaves. A "necessary sacrifice to the establishment of the Constitution" (Rufus King, Mass.). Every slave was counted as only three-fifths of a person in determining representation.

shall be made within three years after the first meeting of the Congress of the United States, and within every subsequent term of ten years, in such manner as they shall by law direct. The number of Representatives shall not exceed one for every thirty thousand, but each State shall have at least one representative; and until such enumeration shall be made, the State of New Hampshire shall be entitled to choose three; Massachusetts, eight; Rhode Island and Providence Plantations, one; Connecticut, five; New York, six; New Jersey, four; Pennsylvania, eight; Delaware, one; Maryland, six; Virginia, ten; North Carolina, five; South Carolina, five; and Georgia, three.

d. Filling vacancies. When vacancies happen in the representation from any State, the Executive authority thereof shall issue writs of election to fill such vacancies.

e. Officers; impeachment. The House of Representatives shall choose their Speaker and other officers; and shall have the sole power of impeachment.

Section 3. **The Senate**

a. Number and election of members. The Senate of the United States shall be composed of two Senators from each state, chosen by the legislature thereof, for six years, and each Senator shall have one vote.

b. Classification. Immediately after they shall be assembled in consequence of the first election, they shall be divided as equally as may be into three classes. The seats of the Senators of the first class shall be vacated at the expiration of the second year, of the second class at the expiration of the fourth year, and of the third class at the expiration of the sixth year, so that one third may be chosen every second year; and if vacancies happen by resignation, or otherwise, during the recess of the legislature of any State, the Executive thereof may make temporary appointments until the next meeting of the legislature, which shall then fill such vacancies.

c. Qualifications of members. No person shall be a Senator who shall not have attained to the age of thirty years, and been nine years a citizen of the United States, and who shall not, when elected, be an inhabitant of that State for which he shall be chosen.

d. President of Senate. The Vice President of the United States shall be President of the Senate, but shall have no vote, unless they be equally divided.

e. Other officers. The Senate shall choose their own officers,

At the eleventh hour, George Washington made his only speech of the convention, urging that the figure be lowered from the original 40,000, increasing representation in the House. Size of the House was set at 435 members in 1929. Each member today represents more than 500,000 people. (Indians, who pay no taxes and who are wards of the government, are still not counted in the apportionment of Representatives.) California has the most Representatives—45; several states have only one.

The House has impeached 15 government officials, including President Andrew Johnson (acquitted by the Senate in 1868) and Supreme Court Associate Justice Samuel Chase (acquitted in 1805).

"A small number was most convenient for deciding on peace and war."—Nathaniel Gorham (Mass.).

Superseded in 1913 by Section 1 of the 17th Amendment. We the People now elect our Senators directly.

Terms of four, seven, nine, or 14 years were rejected.

So there would be experienced Senators during the first years of the Republic.

Changed by the Second Paragraph of the 17th Amendment.

James Madison warned that the numerous poor, rather than the few rich, would someday have the power. Several of his 150 speeches vigorously opposed concession of equality in the Senate to the small states.

Senator-elect Albert Gallatin was barred in 1793, because he allegedly had not been a citizen long enough. Henry Clay (Ky.) was underage when elected to the Senate but the required minimum age of 30 when he took office.

Presiding over the Senate, John Adams cast the most tie-breaking votes, 29. Ten Vice Presidents never cast a vote. Control of the Senate has changed hands 23 times, most recently in 1987.

and also a President pro tempore, in the absence of the Vice President, or when he shall exercise the office of President of the United States.

f. Trial of impeachment. The Senate shall have the sole power to try all impeachments. When sitting for that purpose, they shall be on oath or affirmation. When the President of the United States is tried, the Chief Justice shall preside; and no person shall be convicted without the concurrence of two thirds of the members present.

g. Judgment in case of conviction. Judgment in cases of impeachment shall not extend further than to removal from office, and disqualification to hold and enjoy any office of honor, trust or profit under the United States; but the party convicted shall nevertheless be liable and subject to indictment, trial, judgment and punishment, according to law.

Section 4. How Senators and Representatives Shall Be Chosen and When They Are to Meet

a. Method of holding elections. The times, places and manner of holding elections for Senators and Representatives shall be prescribed in each State by the Legislature thereof; but the Congress may at any time by law make or alter such regulations, except as to the places of choosing Senators.

b. Meeting of Congress. The Congress shall assemble at least once in every year, and such meeting shall be on the first Monday in December, unless they shall by law appoint a different day.

Section 5. Rules of Procedure

a. Organization. Each house shall be the judge of the elections, returns and qualifications of its own members, and a majority of each shall constitute a quorum to do business; but a smaller number may adjourn from day to day, and may be authorized to compel the attendance of absent members, in such manner, and under such penalties, as each house may provide.

b. Rules of proceedings. Each house may determine the rules of its proceedings, punish its members for disorderly behavior, and, with the concurrence of two thirds, expel a member.

c. Journal. Each house shall keep a journal of its proceedings, and from time to time publish the same, excepting such parts as may in their judgment require secrecy; and the yeas and nays of the members of either house on any question shall, at the desire of one-fifth of those present, be entered on the journal.

The only mention of the office of Chief Justice in the Constitution.

Conviction elevates the Vice President into the Oval Office.

The Senate has convicted only five persons, all judges, who were then removed from office.

A property qualification for office-holding—"a veneration of wealth"—was rejected by the delegates.

The 17th Amendment laid down a new method for choosing Senators.

There was no need to meet annually. Rufus King (Mass.) averred: "Too much legislating was a great vice."

Changed to January 20 by Section 2 of the 20th Amendment.

Under the Articles of Confederation, nine of the 13 states had to concur in all important decisions. A quorum was seven states.

The Articles' stipulation that "no person shall be capable of being a delegate for more than three years in any term of six years" restricted the quality of Congressional membership, but it was important for rotation in office.

The Senate met behind closed doors in its first five years.

The people had a "right to know what their agents are doing or have done . . ."—James Wilson (Pa.). The Journals of both chambers have been published together in the *Congressional Record* since 1873.

Details of the convention were kept secret for 50 years. What we know of the proceedings comes principally from James Madison's prodigious notetaking from . . . "a seat in front of the presiding member with the other members on my right and left hands." Our fourth President allowed his journals to be published only posthumously—he was the convention's last survivor (d. 1836).

d. Adjournment. Neither house, during the session of Congress, shall, without the consent of the other, adjourn for more than three days, nor to any other place than that in which the two houses shall be sitting.

Section 6. Compensation, Privileges, and Restrictions

a. Pay and privileges of members. The Senators and Representatives shall receive a compensation for their services, to be ascertained by law, and paid out of the Treasury of the United States. They shall in all cases except treason, felony and breach of the peace, be privileged from arrest during their attendance at the session of their respective houses, and in going to and returning from the same; and for any speech or debate in either house, they shall not be questioned in any other place.

b. Holding other offices prohibited. No Senator or Representative shall, during the time for which he was elected, be appointed to any civil office under the authority of the United States which shall have been created, or the emoluments whereof shall have been increased during such time; and no person holding any office under the United States shall be a member of either house during his continuance in office.

Section 7. Mode of Passing Laws

a. Revenue bills. All bills for raising revenue shall originate in the House of Representatives; but the Senate may propose or concur with amendments as on other bills.

b. How bills become laws. Every bill which shall have passed the House of Representatives and the Senate shall, before it become a law, be presented to the President of the United States; if he approve he shall sign it, but if not he shall return it, with his objections to that house in which it shall have originated, who shall enter the objections at large on their journal, and proceed to reconsider it. If after such reconsideration two-thirds of that house shall agree to pass the bill, it shall be sent, together with the objections, to the other house, by which it shall likewise be reconsidered, and if approved by two-thirds of that house, it shall become a law. But in all such cases the votes of both houses shall be determined by yeas and nays, and the names of the persons voting for and against the bill shall be entered on the journal of each house respectively. If any bill shall not be returned by the President within ten days (Sundays excepted) after it shall have been presented to him, the same shall be a law. in like manner as if he had signed it, unless the

Royal governors had unilaterally suspended and dissolved state assemblies.

To James Madison, it "was an indecent thing and might, in time, prove . . . dangerous . . . to let Congress set its own wages."

Madison, Roger Sherman, Richard Henry Lee, and Elbridge Gerry were among the members of the First Congress. Patrick Henry had successfully blocked Madison's Senatorial candidacy in Virginia.

Congressmen may execute their duties without fear of a civil suit or a criminal prosecution for any cause, including slander or libel. On trumped-up charges, the King used to order the arrest of legislators who opposed his policies.

Rarely is the generic "he" (rather than "people" or "persons") used.

Congress can pass a law over a Presidential veto.

Congress by their adjournment prevent its return, in which case it shall not be a law.

c. Approval or disapproval by the President. Every order, resolution, or vote to which the concurrence of the Senate and House of Representatives may be necessary (except on a question of adjournment) shall be presented to the President of the United States; and before the same shall take effect, shall be approved by him, or being disapproved by him, shall be repassed by two-thirds of the Senate and House of Representatives, according to the rules and limitations prescribed in the case of a bill.

Section 8. **Powers Granted to Congress**

The Congress shall have power

a. To lay and collect taxes, duties, imposts, and excises, to pay the debts and provide for the common defence and general welfare of the United States; but all duties, imposts and excises shall be uniform throughout the United States;

b. To borrow money on the credit of the United States;

c. To regulate commerce with foreign nations, and among the several States, and with the Indian tribes;

d. To establish an uniform rule of naturalization, and uniform laws on the subject of bankruptcies throughout the United States;

e. To coin money, regulate the value thereof, and of foreign coin, and fix the standard of weights and measures;

f. To provide for the punishment of counterfeiting the securities and current coin of the United States;

g. To establish post offices and post roads;

h. To promote the progress of science and useful arts by securing for limited times to authors and inventors the exclusive right to their respective writings and discoveries;

i. To constitute tribunals inferior to the Supreme Court;

j. To define and punish piracies and felonies committed on the high seas and offenses against the law of nations;

k. To declare war, grant letters of marque and reprisal, and make rules concerning captures on land and water;

l. To raise and support armies, but no appropriation of money to that use shall be for a longer term than two years;

m. To provide and maintain a navy;

n. To make rules for the government and regulation of the land and naval forces;

o. To provide for calling forth the militia to execute the laws of

The "pocket veto" (from the Latin for "I forbid"). If Congress adjourns during the ten-day period, the President can effectively veto a bill by not signing it—by "putting it in his pocket."

These 18 paragraphs granted urgently needed powers to Congress. The first 17 are called enumerated powers. The last, the famous "elastic clause," refers to implied powers.

President Washington, in a unique exercise of Commander-in-Chief authority, rode as far as Bedford, Pa., with Secretary of the Treasury Alexander Hamilton, as 13,000 militiamen from four states, along with public opinion, crushed the Whiskey Tax rebellion of 1794 and upheld the principle of Federal supremacy. The Constitution worked!

Elimination of the phrase "and emit bills" made it impossible once and for all for states to print their own money.

Commercial disarray led to the downfall of the Confederation. Clause c. has become a fountain of vast federal power.

h. "If a nation expects to be ignorant and free in a state of civilization," Thomas Jefferson said, "it expects what never was and never will be." The Constitutional Convention defeated the motion to empower Congress "to establish an University, in which no preferences or distinctions should be allowed on account of religion."

k. Originally "make war." So the President's hands would not be tied in case of attack, the convention changed the phrase to a more precise "declare war." The first legislation defining the President's constitutional power to make war was the War Powers Act, which Congress passed over President Richard M. Nixon's veto, in 1973.

the Union, suppress insurrections, and repel invasions;

p. To provide for organizing, arming and disciplining the militia, and for governing such part of them as may be employed in the service of the United States, reserving to the States respectively the appointment of the officers, and the authority of training the militia according to the discipline prescribed by Congress;

q. To exercise exclusive legislation in all cases whatsoever, over such district (not exceeding ten miles square) as may, by cession of particular States, and the acceptance of Congress, become the seat of the government of the United States, and to exercise like authority over all places purchased by the consent of the legislature of the State, in which the same shall be, for the erection of forts, magazines, arsenals, dock-yards, and other needful buildings;—and

r. To make all laws which shall be necessary and proper for carrying into execution the foregoing powers, and all other powers vested by this Constitution in the government of the United States, or in any department or officer thereof.

Section 9. **Powers Denied to the Federal Government**

a. The migration or importation of such persons as any of the States now existing shall think proper to admit, shall not be prohibited by the Congress prior to the year one thousand eight hundred and eight, but a tax or duty may be imposed on such importation, not exceeding ten dollars for each person.

b. The privilege of the writ of habeas corpus shall not be suspended, unless when in cases of rebellion or invasion the public safety may require it.

c. No bill of attainder or ex post facto law shall be passed.

d. No capitation, or other direct, tax shall be laid, unless in proportion to the census or enumeration herein before directed to be taken.

e. No tax or duty shall be laid on articles exported from any State.

f. No preference shall be given by any regulation of commerce or revenue to the ports of one State over those of another: nor shall vessels bound to, or from, one State be obliged to enter, clear, or pay duties in another.

g. No money shall be drawn from the Treasury, but in consequence of appropriations made by law; and a regular statement and account of the receipts and expenditures of all public money shall be published from time to time.

p. Designed to overcome the shortcomings of the militia in the Revolutionary War.

r. The "elastic clause" was a sweeping grant of power, little noticed when enacted, to enable Congress to pass legislation giving effect to the specified powers.

"Infernal traffic," declared George Mason, author of Virginia's Bill of Rights. Mason was one of the three delegates who would "sooner chop off his right hand than put it to the Constitution" in its final form.

Originally 1800.

The political decision to extend slavery was "inconsistent with the principles of the Revolution and [it was] dishonorable to the American character to have such a feature in the Constitution," asserted Luther Martin, the Maryland delegate who quit Philadelphia and bitterly contested his state's ratification of the Constitution. Ineluctable necessity was said to have justified the intractable evil of slavery.

b. The rule of habeas corpus—literally, "you must have the body"—is a foundation of all free societies. An arrested person must be produced in court to determine the justice of his detention. President Abraham Lincoln suspended this sovereign right, arguably violating the Constitution "to save it." Via the same tenet and pretext under which dictators suspend constitutions, our first "constitutional dictator" felt that "measures, however unconstitutional, might become lawful by becoming indispensable to the preservation of the Constitution through the preservation of the nation."

d. The 16th Amendment gives Congress the power to tax incomes, thus modifying the "no capitation" (tax on each person) clause. The slave states had feared a tax on their "three-fifths of all other persons."

e. A concession to the South. Denying this power common to governments at the time took "from government half the regulation of trade."—(James Wilson, Pa.).

f. Allayed Maryland's fear that traffic on Chesapeake Bay would have to enter or clear at a Virginia port to simplify the collection of duties.

h. No title of nobility shall be granted by the United States: and no person holding any office of profit or trust under them shall, without the consent of the Congress, accept of any present, emolument, office, or title, of any kind whatever, from any king, prince, or foreign state.

Section 10. Powers Denied to the States

a. No State shall enter into any treaty, alliance, or confederation; grant letters of marque and reprisal; coin money; emit bills of credit; make any thing but gold and silver coin a tender in payment of debts; pass any bill of attainder, ex post facto law, or law impairing the obligation of contracts, or grant any title of nobility.

b. No State shall, without the consent of the Congress, lay any imposts or duties on imports or exports, except what may be absolutely necessary for executing its inspection laws; and the net produce of all duties and imposts, laid by any State on imports or exports, shall be for the use of the treasury of the United States; and all such laws shall be subject to the revision and control of the Congress.

c. No State shall, without the consent of Congress, lay any duty of tonnage, keep troops, or ships of war in time of peace, enter into any agreement or compact with another State, or with a foreign power, or engage in war, unless actually invaded, or in such imminent danger as will not admit of delay.

Article 2

EXECUTIVE DEPARTMENT

Section 1. President and Vice President

a. Term of office. The executive power shall be vested in a President of the United States of America. He shall hold his office during the term of four years, and together with the Vice President, chosen for the same term, be elected as follows:

b. Electors. Each State shall appoint, in such manner as the legislature thereof may direct, a number of electors, equal to the whole number of Senators and Representatives to which the State may be entitled in the Congress; but no Senator or Representative, or person holding an office of trust or profit under the United States, shall be appointed an elector.

Former method of electing President and Vice President. The electors shall meet in their respective States, and vote by ballot

a. The framers had lived through the disaster of the Continental dollar. (Today's fiscal conservatives argue that this country's economic problems are a direct consequence of the Supreme Court's failure to uphold the monetary provisions of the Constitution.)

This provision was aimed at the welter of state laws favoring debtors over creditors.

The First Congress represented the people beyond their best hopes. It organized the three branches of government, regulated foreign commerce, created a national bank and the national judiciary system, admitted the states of Vermont and Kentucky, initiated the Constitutional amendment process, established the census, funded the national debt, and dealt with petitions for increased tariffs on imported mustard, paint, cordage, and cotton clothes, and with Quaker demands to end slavery.

The state militia was to bear the brunt until Congress could act. During Washington's two-term Presidency, the U.S. army grew from 840 men to 7,108 men.

There were proposals to have the Chief Executive addressed as "His Excellency" or "His Highness," though anti-monarchical sentiment ran deep.

Into the last month, delegates favored a single term of seven years, and there was talk of a three-headed Presidency. Governor Edmund Randolph (Va.) saw the single executive as the "fetus of monarchy."

The office of Vice President was first discussed in the penultimate week of the convention. (Only four states had a Vice President or a Lieutenant Governor.) The position is "hardly worth a pitcher of warm spit." —Vice President John N. Garner (1933–41).

Superseded by the 12th Amendment.

The convention needed 60 ballots to decide on the method of selecting the President.

for two persons, of whom one at least shall not be an inhabitant of the same State with themselves. And they shall make a list of all the persons voted for, and of the number of votes for each; which list they shall sign and certify, and transmit sealed to the seat of government of the United States, directed to the President of the Senate. The President of the Senate shall, in the presence of the Senate and House of Representatives, open all the certificates, and the votes shall then be counted. The person having the greatest number of votes shall be the President, if such number be a majority of the whole number of electors appointed; and if there be more than one who have such majority, and have an equal number of votes, then the House of Representatives shall immediately choose by ballot one of them for President; and if no person have a majority, then from the five highest on the list the said house shall in like manner choose the President. But in choosing the President the votes shall be taken by States, the representation from each State having one vote; a quorum for this purpose shall consist of a member or members from two-thirds of the States, and a majority of all the States shall be necessary to a choice. In every case, after the choice of the President, the person having the greatest number of votes of the electors shall be the Vice President. But if there should remain two or more who have equal votes, the Senate shall choose from them by ballot the Vice President.

c. Time of elections. The Congress may determine the time of choosing the electors, and the day on which they shall give their votes; which day shall be the same throughout the United States.

d. Qualifications of the President. No person except a natural born citizen, or a citizen of the United States, at the time of the adoption of this Constitution, shall be eligible to the office of President; neither shall any person be eligible to that office who shall not have attained to the age of thirty-five years, and been fourteen years a resident within the United States.

e. Vacancy. In case of the removal of the President from office or of his death, resignation, or inability to discharge the powers and duties of the said office, the same shall devolve on the Vice President, and the Congress may by law provide for the case of removal, death, resignation, or inability, both of the President and Vice President, declaring what officer shall then act as President, and such officer shall act accordingly, until the disability be removed, or a President shall be elected.

f. The President's salary. The President shall, at stated times, receive for his services, a compensation, which shall neither be

In 1820, one elector (William Plumer, of New Hampshire) deliberately cast the lone ballot for Secretary of State John Quincy Adams, so James ("Era of Good Feelings") Monroe would not blemish George Washington's unique record of having been elected President unanimously. (Washington was *twice!*)

This Clause Has Been Affected by the 25th Amendment.

Our first President, who had sailed across New York harbor for his inauguration to the strains of "God Save the King," walked on untrodden ground: "There is scarcely any part of my conduct which may not hereafter be drawn into precedent."

Until 1845, each state set its own date for Presidential elections. The 538 electors today vote on the first Monday after the second Wednesday in December following the election. Congress counts the ballots at the end of the first week in January. Of 17,000 electoral votes cast in our history, there have been only about 10 faithless electors.

The electoral college is said to be a paradigm of the American democracy, because it is based on popular votes aggregated state by state. With only 39 percent of the popular vote, but the most of all candidates, third-party aspirant George Wallace netted 100 percent of Arkansas' electoral vote in 1968. It's winner take all.

Benjamin Harrison became President via the electoral college, though he lost the popular vote (by 0.8 percent) to Grover Cleveland. James Garfield defeated W. S. Hancock for the Presidency by a mere 9,457 popular votes, yet won 57.9 percent of the electoral vote.

Not merely requiring "maturity" or "adequate age"—35 is about as specific as one can get.

The first statute enacted under the Constitution set forth the oaths to be administered to all Federal officeholders except the President.

increased nor diminished during the period for which he shall have been elected, and he shall not receive within that period any other emolument from the United States, or any of them.
g. Oath of office. Before he enter on the execution of his office, he shall take the following oath or affirmation:—"I do solemnly swear (or affirm) that I will faithfully execute the office of President of the United States, and will to the best of my ability, preserve, protect and defend the Constitution of the United States."

Section 2. **Powers of the President**

a. Military powers; reprieves and pardons. The President shall be commander in chief of the army and navy of the United States, and of the militia of the several States, when called into the actual service of the United States; he may require the opinion, in writing, of the principal officer in each of the executive departments, upon any subject relating to the duties of their respective offices, and he shall have power to grant reprieves and pardons for offences against the United States, except in cases of impeachment.

b. Treaties; appointments. He shall have power, by and with the advice and consent of the Senate, to make treaties, provided two-thirds of the Senators present concur; and he shall nominate, and by and with the advice and consent of the Senate, shall appoint ambassadors, other public ministers and consuls, judges of the Supreme Court, and all other officers of the United States, whose appointments are not herein otherwise provided for, and which shall be established by law: but the Congress may by law vest the appointment of such inferior officers as they think proper, in the President alone, in the courts of law, or in the heads of departments.

c. Filling vacancies. The President shall have power to fill up all vacancies that may happen during the recess of the Senate, by granting commissions which shall expire at the end of their next session.

Section 3. **Duties of the President**

He shall from time to time give to the Congress information of the state of the Union, and recommend to their consideration such measures as he shall judge necessary and expedient; he may, on extraordinary occasions, convene both houses, or either of them, and in case of disagreement between them with respect to the time of adjournment, he may adjourn them to

The Constitution makes no provision for the Vice President's oath, and it does not stipulate who shall administer the oath to either the President or the Vice President. John Adams was sworn as our first Vice President several days before President-elect George Washington even had arrived in New York for *his* inauguration. No President, and only one Vice President, has been sworn outside the U.S.

This led to the Presidential cabinet. The convention did not vote on a late August proposal that the President "shall have a privy council" (eight states had one advising the governor). The word "cabinet" was never mentioned.

The one explicit reference to bureaucracy.

There have been at least 13 Congressional resolutions to change the way Supreme Court Justices are chosen.

In 1789, John Jay was appointed by President Washington to be the nation's first Chief Justice. Three years earlier, Jay, as Secretary for Foreign Affairs, had urged Congress to give up navigational rights on the Mississippi River to Spain in return for Eastern "commercial advantages." The proposal infuriated Southerners and Westerners.

The Jay Treaty (1794–95), negotiated In London by Chief Justice John Jay, averted war: Britain would withdraw its troops from the Northwest Territory and an arbitration commission would settle debts between the two countries. The (Thomas Pinckney) Treaty of San Lorenzo with Spain (1795) established the Mississippi as the nation's Western boundary, and the U.S. gained free navigation on the river and the right of deposit at New Orleans. (Jay returned from London to learn that without even campaigning he'd been voted into New York's governorship.)

Between John Adams and Woodrow Wilson, no President made an appearance before Congress.

Until 1893, the U.S. was represented abroad only by ministries or consulates. Ambassadors were still considered a device of monarchies.

such time as he shall think proper; he shall receive ambassadors and other public ministers; he shall take care that the laws be faithfully executed, and shall commission all the officers of the United States.

Section 4. Impeachment

The President, Vice President and all civil officers of the United States shall be removed from office on impeachment for, and conviction of, treason, bribery, or other high crimes and misdemeanors.

Article 3

JUDICIAL DEPARTMENT

Section 1. The Federal Courts

The judicial power of the United States shall be vested in one Supreme Court, and in such inferior courts as the Congress may from time to time ordain and establish. The judges, both of the Supreme and inferior courts, shall hold their offices during good behavior, and shall, at stated times, receive for their services, a compensation, which shall not be diminished during their continuance in office.

Section 2. Jurisdiction of the Federal Courts

a. Federal courts in general. The judicial power shall extend to all cases, in law and equity, arising under this Constitution, the laws of the United States, and treaties made or which shall be made, under their authority;—to all cases affecting ambassadors, other public ministers and consuls;—to all cases of admiralty and maritime jurisdiction;—to controversies to which the United States shall be a party;—to controversies between two or more States;—between a State and citizens of another State;—between citizens of different States;—between citizens of the same State claiming lands under grants of different States, and between a State, or the citizens thereof, and foreign states, citizens or subjects.
b. Supreme Court. In all cases affecting ambassadors, other public ministers and consuls, and those in which a State shall be a party, the Supreme Court shall have original jurisdiction. In all the other cases before mentioned, the Supreme Court shall have appellate jurisdiction, both as to law and fact, with such

G. Morris: "The President must not be impeachable."
B. Franklin: "Well, he'd either be impeachable or he'd be assassinated."
G. Morris: "My opinion has changed."

Three articles of impeachment against President Richard M. Nixon were approved by the House Judiciary Committee after Mr. Nixon obeyed the Supreme Court's unanimous decision that he must surrender White House tape recordings pertaining to the infamous break-in of the Democratic National Committee headquarters in Washington, D.C. Faced with overwhelming evidence, Mr. Nixon resigned on August 9, 1974.

"God save the United States and this honorable Court" is how the Supreme Court is called to order. The Court is "a continuing Constitutional Convention."

In *Marbury* v. *Madison* (1803), Chief Justice John Marshall declared that the Court had the power of judicial review. It could decide what the Constitution meant and find unconstitutional and unenforceable a Federal law or action not in agreement with it. The Supreme Court would have the last word.

The first Supreme Court case of consequence concerned the pension claims of veterans of the Revolutionary War. At first, the Court had six members, who met infrequently and in taverns in New York and Philadelphia; later, it convened in a remote basement room in the north wing of the Capitol. The Constitution says nothing about the size of the Court. There have been as many as 10 members. The lifetime appointment of the Chief Justice has been considered to have a greater historical impact than the Presidency. There have been 16 Chief Justices—first among equals—and 103 Justices. Twenty-four nominees have been rejected by the Senate. As the country grew, more Justices were added to the Court to help ride the circuits. One President, William Howard Taft (1909–13), became the 10th Chief Justice (1921–30), appointed by President Warren G. Harding. Charles Evans Hughes resigned as Associate Justice in 1916 to run as the Republican Presidential candidate against the incumbent, Woodrow Wilson. In 1930, Hughes was named Taft's successor as Chief Justice by President Herbert Hoover.

Parts of This Section Were Altered by the 11th Amendment.

exceptions, and under such regulations as the Congress shall make.

c. Rules respecting trials. The trial of all crimes, except in cases of impeachment, shall be by jury; and such trial shall be held in the State where the said crimes shall have been committed; but when not committed within any State, the trial shall be at such place or places as the Congress may by law have directed.

Section 3. Treason

a. Definition of treason. Treason against the United States shall consist only in levying war against them, or in adhering to their enemies, giving them aid and comfort. No person shall be convicted of treason unless on the testimony of two witnesses to the same overt act, or on confession in open court.

b. Punishment of treason. The Congress shall have power to declare the punishment of treason, but no attainder of treason shall work corruption of blood, or forfeiture except during the life of the person attainted.

Article 4

THE STATES AND THE FEDERAL GOVERNMENT

Section 1. State Records

Full faith and credit shall be given in each State to the public acts, records, and judicial proceedings of every other State. And the Congress may by general laws prescribe the manner in which such acts, records, and proceedings shall be proved, and the effect thereof.

Section 2. Privileges and Immunities of Citizens

a. Privileges. The citizens of each State shall be entitled to all privileges and immunities of citizens in the several States.

b. Extradition. A person charged in any State with treason, felony, or other crime, who shall flee from justice, and be found in another State, shall, on demand of the executive authority of the State from which he fled, be delivered up, to be removed to the State having jurisdiction of the crime.

c. Fugitive workers. No person held to service or labor in one State, under the laws thereof, escaping into another shall in consequence of any law or regulation therein, be discharged

Fewer than 200 of the 5,000 annual requests receive a full hearing from the Supreme Court today.

The Court lacks the power of the purse or the sword, and relies on the elected branches to enforce its decisions. (Alexander Hamilton, *Federalist* No. 78.)

The only crime defined in the Constitution. Former Vice President Aaron Burr was acquitted of treason (1807) when President Thomas Jefferson's Federal prosecutors could not prove the charge. Talking or thinking about committing a treasonable act is not considered treason in the United States.

Congress may not attempt to exercise powers assigned to the executive and the judicial departments.

This is the only time the states are referred to by a plural pronoun.

The next generation will not be penalized.

"Without [the Judges'] active cooperation, the Constitution would be a dead letter."—Alexis de Tocqueville.

Acts required of the states and drawn from the Articles of Confederation.

By this so-called "friendship clause," the states recognize one another's contracts, wills, and civil judgements.

c. Superseded by the 13th Amendment. In 1857, Chief Justice Roger Brooke Taney declared that blacks were not people but "articles of merchandise." He invalidated the Missouri Compromise and made the Civil War all but inevitable.

from such service or labor, but shall be delivered up on claim of the party to whom such service or labor may be due.

Section 3. New States and Territories

a. Admission of new States. New States may be admitted by the Congress into this Union; but no new State shall be formed or erected within the jurisdiction of any other State; nor any State be formed by the junction of two or more States, or parts of States, without the consent of the legislatures of the States concerned, as well as of the Congress.

b. Power of Congress over territory and property. The Congress shall have power to dispose of and make all needful rules and regulations respecting the territory or other property belonging to the United States; and nothing in this Constitution shall be so construed as to prejudice any claims of the United States, or of any particular State.

Section 4. Guarantees to the States

The United States shall guarantee to every State in this Union a republican form of government, and shall protect each of them against invasion; and on application of the legislature or of the executive (when the legislature cannot be convened) against domestic violence.

Article 5

METHOD OF AMENDMENT

The Congress, whenever two-thirds of both houses shall deem it necessary, shall propose amendments to this Constitution, or, on the application of the legislatures of two-thirds of the several States, shall call a convention for proposing amendments, which, in either case shall be valid to all intents and purposes, as part of this Constitution, when ratified by the legislatures of three-fourths of the several States, or by conventions in three-fourths thereof, as the one or the other mode of ratification may be proposed by the Congress; provided that no amendments which may be made prior to the year one thousand eight hundred and eight shall in any manner affect the first and fourth clauses in the ninth section of the first article, and that no State, without its consent, shall be deprived of its equal suffrage in the Senate.

The fugitive slave clause, a Southern proposal, was not sanctioned under the Articles of Confederation. It was part of the historic Northwest Ordinance. But by 1860, slavery had become a national institution, legal wherever not forbidden by state law, and it had considerable Federal protection.

The U.S. from the Alleghenies to the Mississippi River was far larger in area than the 13 states. Eastern delegates argued strenuously against equality for new states. During the convention, the Continental Congress back in New York was accomplishing its most memorable work: adoption of the Northwest Ordinance, based on a plan drafted earlier by Thomas Jefferson. The 6.5-million-square-mile territory North of the Ohio River would be divided into three to five states—with admission to the Union in full equality to the original states—and (to Southern huzzahs) slavery would be barred so competing tobacco and indigo would not be produced there. (The Congress transacted its last official business on October 10, 1788, three and a half months after the new Constitution had been adopted.)

No action has ever been taken under this clause.

Adopted in the last week of the convention to head off any amendment banning slave trade sooner. "South Carolina and Georgia cannot do without slaves."—C. C. Pinckney (So. Carolina).

The only amendment that can't be proposed. The clause was adopted to head off Roger Sherman's concern that "three-fourths of the states might be brought to do things fatal to particular states, such as abolishing them altogether or depriving them of their equality in the Senate."

BALANCING THE BUDGET—
THE NEXT AMENDMENT ?

Article 6

GENERAL PROVISIONS

a. Public debt. All debts contracted and engagements entered into, before the adoption of this Constitution, shall be as valid against the United States under this Constitution, as under the Confederation.

b. Supremacy of the Constitution. This Constitution, and the laws of the United States which shall be made in pursuance thereof; and all treaties made, or which shall be made, under the authority of the United States, shall be the supreme law of the land; and the judges in every State shall be bound thereby, anything in the Constitution or laws of any State to the contrary notwithstanding.

c. Oath of office; no religious test. The Senators and Representatives before mentioned, and the members of the several State legislatures, and all executive and judicial officers, both of the United States and of the several States, shall be bound by oath or affirmation, to support this Constitution; but no religious test shall ever be required as a qualification to any office or public trust under the United States.

Article 7

RATIFICATION OF THE CONSTITUTION

The ratification of the conventions of nine States shall be sufficient for the establishment of this Constitution between the States so ratifying the same.

Done in Convention by the unanimous consent of the States present the Seventeenth Day of September in the Year of our Lord one thousand seven hundred and eighty seven and of the Independence of the United States of America the Twelfth. In Witness whereof We have hereunto subscribed our Names.

G. Washington
Presidt and deputy from Virginia

New Hampshire
John Langdon
Nicholas Gilman

Massachusetts
Nathaniel Gorham
Rufus King

Delaware
Geo: Read
John Dickinson
Jaco: Broom
Gunning Bedford Jr.
Richard Bassett

34

It is counterbalanced by the 10th Amendment.

Introduced by the mercurial Governor Edmund Randolph, it's been disclaimed by some as "legal robbery, such as the history of civilized nations can scarcely produce a parallel to." Pierce Butler (S.C.) was concerned that redemption of government paper at face value would succor the "bloodsuckers who had speculated on the distresses of others . . ." The question of full or partial redemption was left unresolved.

The important clause, lifted from the Magna Carta, was prompted by Congress' demand that states repeal laws violating the Treaty of Paris. States cannot pass laws contrary to the Constitution. The principle of Federal supremacy was tested in the Whiskey Rebellion (1794), and again in South Carolina's Ordinance of Nullification (1832) declaring void the Tariff Acts of 1828 and 1832, and again of course in the Civil War.

Adopted unanimously by the delegates, though 11 of the states had a religious qualification for state representatives. Many also required voters to own property and officeholders to be well off. Nowhere does the Constitution actually speak of separation of church and state. That there was no religious test provided ample ammunition for anti-Constitutionalists during the ratification process. God is not mentioned anywhere in the Constitution (but *is* in the Declaration of Independence).

Reinforces the "supreme law of the land" clause. But three-quarters of a century later, a great many people still felt loyalty to the state rather than to the nation. The West Point star graduate Robert E. Lee, for one, elected to defend Virginia and the Confederacy, although he opposed slavery and secession.

Twenty-three Articles were condensed into seven by Gouverneur Morris (Pa.) and the Committee of Style. Article 7 is the only original Article with no present-day significance.

Proposed re-dividing the country and making every state the same size.

The Constitution was not free from imperfections, Washington said, but "beyond any thing we had a right to imagine or expect."

Nathaniel Gorham presided when the convention met in the Committee of the Whole; Washington would then sit with the Virginia delegation.

Connecticut
Wm. Saml Johnson
Roger Sherman

New York
Alexander Hamilton

New Jersey
Wil: Livingston
David Brearley
Wm. Paterson
Jona: Dayton

Pennsylvania
B. Franklin
Robt. Morris
Thos. FitzSimons
James Wilson
Thomas Mifflin
Geo. Clymer
Jared Ingersoll
Gouv Morris

Maryland
James McHenry
Danl. Carroll
Dan: of St. Thos. Jenifer

Virginia
John Blair
James Madison Jr.

North Carolina
Wm. Blount
Hu Williamson
Richd Dobbs Spaight

South Carolina
J. Rutledge
Charles Pinckney
Charles Cotesworth Pinckney
Pierce Butler

Georgia
William Few
Abr. Baldwin

Attest:
William Jackson, *Secretary.*

In Convention Monday, September 17th, 1787.

Resolved,

That the preceding Constitution be laid before the United States in Congress assembled, and that it is the Opinion of this Convention, that it should afterwards be submitted to a Convention of Delegates, chosen in each State by the People thereof, under the Recommendation of its Legislature, for their Assent and Ratification; and that each Convention assenting to, and ratifying the Same, should give Notice thereof to the United States in Congress assembled.

Resolved, That it is the Opinion of this Convention, that as soon as the Conventions of nine States shall have ratified this Constitution, the United States in Congress assembled should fix a Day on which Electors should be appointed by the States which shall have ratified the same, and a Day on which the Electors should assemble to vote for the President, and the Time and Place for commencing Proceedings under this Constitution. . . . . By the Unanimous Order of the Convention.

Benjamin Franklin said, "I confess, that I do not entirely approve of this Constitution at present; but, Sir, I am not sure I shall never approve it; for, having lived long, I have experienced many instances of being obliged, by better information or fuller consideration, to change my opinions even on important subjects, which I once thought right, but I found to be otherwise . . . I consent, Sir, to this Constitution, because I expect no better, and because I am not sure that it is not the best."

As an independent Tennessee Senator, he became the subject of the United States' first impeachment trial, for conspiring with the British against Spanish Florida. In all, 15 Senators have been expelled.

A 44-year-old golf-playing continentalist, he influenced the design of the Presidency. Wilson was steeped in constitution theory and law, his mind one blaze of light. Later, he owned 4,000,000 acres, and though a Supreme Court Justice he jumped bail in a debtor's case and became a fugitive.

"Tall Boy"—an arrogant ladies' man with a peg leg—delivered 173 speeches, more than any other delegate, though he missed a full month of sessions. He was the principal drafter of the final document.

The only other formal nominee for Secretary was Benjamin Franklin's grandnephew William Temple Franklin. Jackson carried the document to Congress, in New York, which eight days later agreed to transmit it to the states.

Congress was not asked for its approval of the proposed Constitution, and didn't give it, but if Congress had decided not to send the Constitution to the states, there wasn't much its framers could have done. Ratification would be decided by "We the People" in convention state by state rather than by potentially hostile state legislatures, whose powers would be clipped by the Constitution.

Just after the convention, James Madison said that "the document would neither effectually answer its national object nor prevent the local mischiefs which everywhere excite disgusts against state governments."

Eleven days after the Constitution had been signed by barely over half the delegates appointed months earlier, a reluctant Confederation Congress, prodded by a fatigued James Madison, agreed to submit the proposed Constitution to state ratifying conventions called by the legislatures. The anti-Federalists, or Grumbletonians, argued that the "secret, dark cabal" did not abide by Congress' directive only to revise the Articles of Confederation. The people, they claimed, didn't want 13 pillars struck down in favor of one colossus. Trading the Articles for a new charter without a Bill of Rights was preposterous. Mercy Otis Warren—the "Columbian Patriot"—argued heatedly that the "fraudulent usurpation at Philadelphia" would "draw blood from every pore by taxes, impositions, and illegal restrictions." To record a comprehensive, reasoned, and candid defense of the new Constitution, Alexander Hamilton, James Madison, and John Jay—under the pseudonym "Publius" and the title *The Federalist*—dashed off 85 newspaper essays, hailed today as the authoritative commentary on the American system of government. Madison believed a second convention, desired by the opposition, would "give opportunities to designing men which it might be impossible to counteract." The Federalists delivered a master stroke: "rights" amendments would be proposed in the First Congress to assuage the fears of the people.

The Constitution became the supreme law of the land with the ninth state's ratification—New Hampshire's—in June, 1788. Four days later, without knowledge of New Hampshire's adoption, Governor Edmund Randolph, a former anti-Federalist who had not signed the Constitution, collaborated with Madison, John Marshall, and other Federalists to bring in Virginia. Without ratification, Randolph declared, "the Union will be dissolved, the dogs of war will break loose, and anarchy and discord will complete the ruin of this country." (Until North Carolina and Rhode Island, grudgingly, ratified the Constitution, they were treated like foreign nations and even faced the threat of import duties on their goods.)

On March 4, 1789, the new government convened: eight (of 22) Senators and 13 (of 59) Representatives were present. It took another month for Congress to muster quorums.

Wearing a dark brown suit of superfine American Broad Cloths bought through an advertisement, white stockings, shoes with silver buckles, and a steel-hilted dress sword, George Washington was sworn as Chief Executive on a portico of the Doric-columned Federal Hall in New York, the nation's capital, on April 30. On September 24,

Congress passed the Judiciary Act of 1789 establishing a Supreme Court, 13 district courts, and three circuit courts. The next day, Congress submitted for the states' approval a dozen amendments to the two-year-old Constitution.

About 10,000 amendments have been introduced in Congress; among them are direct election of the President, prohibition of dueling, and military duty by voluntary enlistment only. Thirty-three have been formalized and sent to the states for ratification. The six not adopted by the necessary three-fourths of the states include one amendment in the First Congress's package of a dozen. (The first 10 that were adopted are called collectively the Bill of Rights.) The six are:

1789: concerning the ratio of members in the House of Representatives to population.

1810: concerning the abrogation of citizenship for accepting gifts or titles of nobility from a foreign power without the consent of Congress. It missed adoption by one state.

1861: concerning non-Congressional interference in slavery. Offered to head off the Civil War, it was adopted by only two states. It was the first proposed amendment signed by a President (Buchanan) before distribution to the states. (Just before he was murdered, President Lincoln signed the proposed Thirteenth Amendment.)

1924: concerning the labor of persons under 18 years of age. It was opposed by manufacturing associations and some religious groups.

1972: concerning equality of rights regardless of gender. E.R.A. fell three states short of adoption.

1978: concerning representation of the District of Columbia in the House and the Senate. D.C. has a population larger than do four of the states.

Three new proposals for amendments that are arousing interest would require: a balanced Federal budget; a four-year term for Representatives to coincide with the Presidential term; and modification of the treaty requirement, possibly to a straight majority decision.

AMENDMENTS TO THE CONSTITUTION OF THE UNITED STATES OF AMERICA

(The first 10 Amendments—the Bill of Rights—were ratified in 1791, after 1 year, 2½ months.)

Amendment 1

FREEDOM OF RELIGION, SPEECH, AND THE PRESS; RIGHT OF ASSEMBLY

Congress shall make no law respecting an establishment of religion, or prohibiting the free exercise thereof; or abridging the freedom of speech, or of the press; or the right of the people peaceably to assemble, and to petition the government for a redress of grievances.

Amendment 2

RIGHT TO KEEP AND BEAR ARMS

A well-regulated militia, being necessary to the security of a free State, the right of the people to keep and bear arms, shall not be infringed.

Amendment 3

QUARTERING OF TROOPS

No soldier shall, in time of peace be quartered in any house, without the consent of the owner, nor in time of war, but in a manner to be prescribed by law.

Amendment 4

LIMITING THE RIGHT OF SEARCH

The right of the people to be secure in their persons, houses, papers, and effects, against unreasonable searches and seizures, shall not be violated, and no warrants shall issue but upon probable cause, supported by oath or affirmation, and particularly describing the place to be searched, and the persons or things to be seized.

In 1790, Supreme Court Justice (and convention delegate) James Wilson observed that the Constitution "is clay in the hands of a potter [the people]; they have the right to mold, to preserve, to improve, to refine, and to furnish it as they please."

In the last week of the Constitutional Convention, the 10 states present rejected Elbridge Gerry's and George Mason's bid to appoint a committee to draft a Bill of Rights. Roger Sherman said, "The states' declarations of rights are not repealed by this Constitution, and being in force are quite sufficient." The Bill, it turned out, would have given "great quiet to the people," especially to the anti-Federalists. Its omission was not to Thomas Jefferson's liking, either; from Paris, he urged his friend James Madison to work for a Bill of Rights.

The "majestic generalities" of the first 10 Amendments reserve to the people or to the states powers not delegated to the Federal government. Their adoption headed off a second convention. (About 200 amendments had been proposed in the states' ratifying conventions; 17 were reviewed seriously by the First Congress.)

None of these protected rights can be considered absolute. Mormons, for instance, cannot lawfully extend freedom of religion to the practice of polygamy.

Not until 1962 and 1963 did the Supreme Court declare unconstitutional the practice of requiring children to say prayers and read the Bible in schools.

The 14th Amendment has been construed to extend to the states the prohibitions of the 1st Amendment.

The 3rd Amendment was drawn because the British had forced colonists to take soldiers into their homes. The first case to raise a real issue under this Amendment came in the early 1980s, in connection with the housing of riot-busting National Guardsmen in Sing Sing Prison, in New York State.

The 4th Amendment protects people, not places; it does not outlaw searches. Privacy—"the right most valued by civilized men"—has been implied by judicial decision.

Amendment 5

No person shall be held to answer for a capital, or otherwise infamous crime, unless on a presentment or indictment of a grand jury, except in cases arising in the land or naval forces, or in the militia, when in actual service in time of war or public danger; nor shall any person be subject for the same offense to be twice put in jeopardy of life or limb; nor shall be compelled in any criminal case to be a witness against himself, nor be deprived of life, liberty, or property, without due process of law; nor shall private property be taken for public use, without just compensation.

Amendment 6

RIGHTS OF ACCUSED PERSONS

In all criminal prosecutions, the accused shall enjoy the right to a speedy and public trial, by an impartial jury of the State and district wherein the crime shall have been committed, which districts shall have been previously ascertained by law, and to be informed of the nature and cause of the accusation; to be confronted with the witnesses against him; to have compulsory process for obtaining witnesses in his favor, and to have the assistance of counsel for his defense.

Amendment 7

RULES OF THE COMMON LAW

In suits at common law, where the value in controversy shall exceed twenty dollars, the right of trial by jury shall be preserved, and no fact tried by a jury, shall be otherwise reexamined in any court of the United States than according to the rules of common law.

Amendment 8

EXCESSIVE BAIL, FINES, AND PUNISHMENT PROHIBITED

Excessive bail shall not be required, nor excessive fines imposed, nor cruel and unusual punishments inflicted.

"The safeguards of liberty have frequently been forged in controversies involving not very nice people."—Justice Felix Frankfurter.

A restraint on the Federal government; in the 14th Amendment, it is a restraint upon state governments.

Insistent demands for still more assurance of the jury over the judiciary led to the 6th and 7th Amendments.

In the 1780s, they included quartering and burning at the stake. (The first penitentiary in the U.S. was opened in Walnut Street in Philadelphia by Quakers. They believed a prison sentence could reform criminals.)

Amendment 9

RIGHTS RETAINED BY THE PEOPLE

The enumeration in the Constitution of certain rights shall not be construed to deny or disparage others retained by the people.

Amendment 10

POWERS RESERVED TO STATES AND PEOPLE

The powers not delegated to the United States by the Constitution, nor prohibited by it to the States, are reserved to the States respectively, or to the people.

Amendment 11

(Ratified in 1798, after 3 years, 10 months)

LIMITING THE POWERS OF FEDERAL COURTS

The judicial power of the United States shall not be construed to extend to any suit in law or equity, commenced or prosecuted against one of the United States by citizens of another State, or by citizens or subjects of any foreign state.

Amendment 12

(Ratified in 1804, after 8½ months)

ELECTION OF PRESIDENT AND VICE PRESIDENT

The electors shall meet in their respective States, and vote by ballot for President and Vice President, one of whom, at least, shall not be an inhabitant of the same State with themselves; they shall name in their ballots the person voted for as President, and in distinct ballots the person voted for as Vice President, and they shall make distinct lists of all persons voted for as President, and of all persons voted for as Vice President, and of the number of votes for each, which lists they shall sign and certify, and transmit sealed to the seat of government of the United States, directed to the President of the Senate;—the President of the Senate shall, in the presence of the Senate and House of Representatives, open all the certificates and the votes shall then be counted;—the person having the greatest number of votes for President shall be the President, if such number be a majority of the whole number of electors appointed; and if no person have such majority, then from the persons having the

The Constitution does not pretend to have listed all the specific rights of the people.

The 9th and 10th Amendments are a guarantee of federalism. Article 2 of the Articles of Confederation had provided: "Each state retains its sovereignty, freedom, and independence and every power, jurisdiction and right . . . not . . . expressly delegated to the United States in Congress assembled."

This Amendment of paramount importance limits the Federal government to certain powers. It was framed by Madison's fellow Virginian Richard Henry Lee, who had opposed ratification of the Constitution. (Lee had introduced the resolution in the Continental Congress calling for a declaration of independence.) There are over 50 mentions of the states in the Constitution, either directly or by clear implication.

There have been only 17 Amendments since 1791.

The only Amendment that concerns the judicial branch of the Federal government; these cases are tried now only in state courts. The 11th modifies Article 3, Section 2, Paragraph 1. It was a purely political Amendment introduced the day after the Court had ruled that a citizen of one state had the right to sue another state. The 12th Amendment patches a basic flaw that became apparent. (Political parties had not been anticipated.) Congressional caucuses nominated our first six Presidents. The 12th Amendment was a response to the tie vote in the Jefferson–Burr (same party) conflict in 1800–01. The House needed to cast 36 (!) ballots before Jefferson was elected. Burr became Vice President. (Three years later, the still-disgruntled Vice President murdered Alexander Hamilton in a duel. Hamilton had helped to elect Jefferson and he thwarted Burr's bid for New York's governorship.) Electors now vote for President and Vice President separately. Only once since the adoption of the 12th Amendment has the House had to choose a President, when John Quincy Adams' 1824 election was marked by a breakdown of the two-party system.

highest numbers not exceeding three on the list of those voted for as President, the House of Representatives shall choose immediately, by ballot, the President. But in choosing the President, the votes shall be taken by States, the representation from each State having one vote; a quorum for this purpose shall consist of a member or members from two-thirds of the States, and a majority of all the States shall be necessary to a choice. And if the House of Representatives shall not choose a President whenever the right of choice shall devolve upon them, before the fourth day of March next following, then the Vice President shall act as President, as in the case of the death or other constitutional disability of the President.—The person having the greatest number of votes as Vice President, shall be the Vice President, if such number be a majority of the whole number of electors appointed, and if no person have a majority, then from the two highest numbers on the list, the Senate shall choose the Vice President; a quorum for the purpose shall consist of two-thirds of the whole number of Senators, and a majority of the whole number shall be necessary to a choice. But no person constitutionally ineligible to the office of President shall be eligible to that of Vice President of the United States.

Amendment 13
(Ratified in 1865, after 10½ months)

SLAVERY ABOLISHED

Section 1. **Abolition of Slavery**

Neither slavery nor involuntary servitude, except as a punishment for crime whereof the party shall have been duly convicted, shall exist within the United States, or any place subject to their jurisdiction.

Section 2. **Enforcement**

Congress shall have power to enforce this article by appropriate legislation.

Amendment 14
(Ratified in 1868, after 2 years, 1½ months)

CITIZENSHIP DEFINED

Section 1. **Definition of Citizenship**

All persons born or naturalized in the United States, and subject

Defeated candidates for re-election had to hang around for four months. The "lame duck" clause was superseded by Section 3 of the 20th Amendment.

Fifteen Presidents have polled less than 50 percent of the popular vote, and two have polled fewer votes than their major opponent.

On the Fourth of July, 1854, in Framingham, Mass., the fiery abolitionist William Lloyd Garrison burned a facsimile of the "pro-slavery" Constitution, proclaiming it a "covenant with death and an agreement with hell . . . a compromise with tyranny." Sojourner Truth, the first black woman anti-slavery speaker, declared, "I feel for my rights, but there ain't any there." In 1857, the Supreme Court ruled the Constitution had been written for whites only. Chief Justice Roger B. Taney affirmed, in the Dred Scott case, that blacks were not citizens and "had no rights which the white man was bound to respect" and Congress had no power to outlaw slavery. (The Senate's 29–15 confirmation of Taney, in 1836, was the lowest ratio for a Chief Justice-designate until the Senate's 65–33 approval of William H. Rehnquist, in 1986.)

The Civil War can be thought of as the necessary completion of the Revolution. President Lincoln had considered amortizing slavery over a half century—freeing the blacks immediately, paying their owners later. The 13th Amendment could not have been ratified without the concurrence of the eight slave states whose governments Congress had not recognized earlier in the year. Banning slavery constitutionally was necessary, because Lincoln's Emancipation Proclamation (January 1, 1863) did not prevent Southern states, on re-admission to the Union, from reinstituting slavery.

The ancient political ideal of equality found explicit recognition with ratification of the 14th Amendment, necessary to protect the citizenship of slaves freed after the Civil War.

to the jurisdiction thereof, are citizens of the United States and of the State wherein they reside. No State shall make or enforce any law which shall abridge the privileges or immunities of citizens of the United States; nor shall any State deprive any person of life, liberty, or property, without due process of law; nor deny to any person within its jurisdiction the equal protection of the laws.

Section 2. Apportionment of Representatives

Representatives shall be apportioned among the several States according to their respective numbers, counting the whole number of persons in each State, excluding Indians not taxed. But when the right to vote at any election for the choice of electors for President and Vice President of the United States, Representatives in Congress, the executive and judicial officers of a State, or the members of the legislature thereof, is denied to any of the male inhabitants of such State, being twenty-one years of age, and citizens of the United States, or in any way abridged, except for participation in rebellion, or other crime, the basis of representation therein shall be reduced in the proportion which the number of such male citizens shall bear to the whole number of male citizens twenty-one years of age in such State.

Section 3. Disability Resulting from Insurrection

No person shall be a Senator or Representative in Congress, or Elector of President and Vice President, or hold any office, civil or military, under the United States, or under any State, who, having previously taken an oath, as a member of Congress, or as an officer of the United States, or as a member of any State legislature, or as an executive or judicial officer of any State to support the Constitution of the United States, shall have engaged in insurrection or rebellion against the same, or given aid or comfort to the enemies thereof. But Congress may by a vote of two-thirds of each house, remove such disability.

Section 4. Public Debt of the United States Valid; Confederate Debt Void

The validity of the public debt of the United States, authorized by law, including debts incurred for payment of pensions and bounties for services in suppressing insurrection or rebellion, shall not be questioned. But neither the United States nor any State shall assume or pay any debt or obligation incurred in aid of insurrection or rebellion against the United States, or any

Originally intended for the protection of Negroes, this clause has been used by corporations to protect their property. A corporation is a "person" in the eyes of the law.

Unless the due process clause is construed to include the most important parts of the first eight Amendments, the states would be free, in theory, to establish an official church or to inflict cruel and unusual punishment. The Reagan Administration has argued that the 14th Amendment cannot be used to make the Bill of Rights binding on state governments.

In 1954, the Supreme Court ruled racial segregation in public schools violated the 14th Amendment clause guaranteeing equal protection of the law.

Never enforced, it became moot in the 1960s when the voting rights laws went into effect.

Changed by Section 1 of the 26th Amendment.

This penalty has never been enforced.

Only use of "male" in the Constitution.

Sections 3 and 4 of the 14th Amendment are now obsolete.

No voting requirement was established. The states set terms by which people became qualified to vote.

"Before the Civil War and the 14th Amendment, the United States *were*. After the Civil War, the United States *is*."—Carl Sandburg.

claim for the loss or emancipation of any slave; but all such debts, obligations, and claims shall be held illegal and void.

Section 5. Enforcement

The Congress shall have power to enforce by appropriate legislation the provisions of this article.

Amendment 15

(Ratified in 1870, after 1 year, 1 month)

RIGHT OF SUFFRAGE

Section 1. The Suffrage

The right of citizens of the United States to vote shall not be denied or abridged by the United States or any State on account of race, color, or previous condition of servitude.

Section 2. Enforcement

The Congress shall have power to enforce this article by appropriate legislation.

Amendment 16

(Ratified in 1913, after 3 years, 7½ months)

INCOME TAX

The Congress shall have power to lay and collect taxes on incomes, from whatever source derived, without apportionment among the several States, and without regard to any census or enumeration.

Amendment 17

(Ratified in 1913, after 1 year, ½ month)

DIRECT ELECTION OF SENATORS

a. Election by the people. The Senate of the United States shall be composed of two Senators from each State, elected by the people thereof, for six years; and each Senator shall have one vote. The electors in each State shall have the qualifications requisite for electors of the most numerous branch of the State legislatures.

Invalidates the Confederate debt.

From 1925 on, the Supreme Court has read the 14th Amendment as imposing most guarantees of the Bill of Rights (which restrict the powers of the Federal government) on state and local governments. This is called "incorporation."

This Amendment became necessary because the Supreme Court alone cannot always protect rights guaranteed by the Constitution.

Blacks must not be deprived of the ballot because of their race or because they were slaves. (Some states quickly found other grounds to deny them the vote.)

From 1820, when Maine separated from Massachusetts and joined the Union as a free state to counter slave-state Missouri, until after the Civil War, every new state denied the vote to free blacks.

Only the three Reconstruction Amendments (13, 14, and 15) had numbers assigned to them at the time of ratification.

In the case of Ponca Chief Standing Bear, the U.S. District Court in Omaha, in 1879, established that Native Americans were protected by the Constitution.

The first new Amendment in over four decades made the income tax legal. An individual was now taxed according to the size of his income rather than according to the population of the state in which he happened to live.

A similar proposal in 1826 was not adopted.

b. Vacancies. When vacancies happen in the representation of any State in the Senate, the executive authority of such State shall issue writs of election to fill such vacancies: Provided that the legislature of any State may empower the executive thereof to make temporary appointments until the people fill the vacancies by election as the legislature may direct.

c. Not retroactive. This amendment shall not be so construed as to affect the election or term of any Senator chosen before it becomes valid as part of the Constitution.

Amendment 18
(Ratified in 1919, after 1 year, 1½ months)

NATIONAL PROHIBITION

Section 1. **Prohibition of Intoxicating Liquors**

After one year from the ratification of this article the manufacture, sale, or transportation of intoxicating liquors within, the importation thereof into, or the exportation thereof from the United States and all territory subject to the jurisdiction thereof for beverage purposes is hereby prohibited.

Section 2. **Enforcement**

The Congress and the several States shall have concurrent power to enforce this article by appropriate legislation.

Section 3. **Limited Time for Ratification**

This article shall be inoperative unless it shall have been ratified as an amendment to the Constitution by the legislatures of the several States, as provided in the Constitution, within seven years from the date of the submission hereof to the States by the Congress.

Amendment 19
(Ratified in 1920, after 1 year, 2½ months)

EXTENDING THE VOTE TO WOMEN

Section 1. **Woman Suffrage**

The right of citizens of the United States to vote shall not be denied or abridged by the United States or by any State on account of sex.

Repealed by the 21st Amendment.

"The noble experiment" was the law of the land for thirteen years. (Maine had been dry since 1842.)

Congress initiated a time provision for amendment ratification. Five of the seven proposed amendments rejected by the states did not include a deadline for ratification.

In 1875, the Supreme Court unanimously decided the right of suffrage must result from explicit legislation or Constitutional amendment rather than through interpretation of the Constitution. Beginning in 1878, a Constitutional amendment extending suffrage to women was repeatedly introduced in Congress.

With a flourish of his ordinary steel pen, Secretary of State Bainbridge Colby signed the certificate of ratification for the 19th Amendment, saying, "I say to the women of America, you may fire when you are ready." The ratification ceremony was not witnessed by a photographer—or by a woman. The United States became the sixteenth country to give women the vote nationally. Many states had had women suffrage laws, and in the 1880s, Belva Ann Lockwood, the first woman to practice before the Supreme Court, had twice run seriously for the Presidency. (Testing the 14th Amendment, Susan B. Anthony had cast her illegal vote in Rochester, N.Y., in 1872, for Republican President Ulysses S. Grant.)

Section 2. **Enforcement**

The Congress shall have power to enforce this article by appropriate legislation.

Amendment 20
(Ratified in 1933, after 11 months)

BEGINNING OF PRESIDENTIAL AND CONGRESSIONAL TERMS

Section 1. **Terms of President, Vice President, and Congress**

The terms of the President and Vice President shall end at noon on the 20th day of January, and the terms of Senators and Representatives at noon on the 3d day of January, of the years in which such terms would have ended if this article had not been ratified; and the terms of their successors shall then begin.

Section 2. **Sessions of Congress**

The Congress shall assemble at least once in every year, and such meeting shall begin at noon on the 3d day of January, unless they shall by law appoint a different day.

Section 3. **Presidential Succession**

If, at the time fixed for the beginning of the term of the President, the President elect shall have died, the Vice President elect shall become President. If a President shall not have been chosen before the time fixed for the beginning of his term, or if the President elect shall have failed to qualify, then the Vice President elect shall act as President until a President shall have qualified; and the Congress may by law provide for the case wherein neither a President elect nor a Vice President elect shall have qualified, declaring who shall then act as President, or the manner in which one who is to act shall be selected, and such person shall act accordingly until a President or Vice President shall have qualified.

Section 4. **Choice of President by the House**

The Congress may by law provide for the case of the death of any of the persons from whom the House of Representatives

In 1937, Franklin D. Roosevelt became the first President inaugurated in January rather than in March (or in April, as was George Washington).

Six professional soldiers have been President: Washington, Andrew Jackson, William Henry Harrison, Zachary Taylor, Ulysses S. Grant, and Dwight D. Eisenhower.

It was previously the first Monday in December.

Altered by the 25th Amendment.

During his lame-duck months as President (November, 1860–March, 1861), President James Buchanan could find no support in the Constitution to deal with the secession states, and he believed, "I will be the last President." The 11 Confederate States of America, headed by Constitutional scholar Jefferson Davis, adopted a charter that resembled the U.S.

Constitution. Exceptions included provisions underscoring state sovereignty, recognizing and protecting slavery, and calling for a one-term Presidency of six years. (All living former Presidents favor a six-year one-term Presidency. President Ronald Reagan doesn't.)

may choose a President, whenever the right of choice shall have devolved upon them, and for the case of the death of any of the persons from whom the Senate may choose a Vice President whenever the right of choice shall have devolved upon them.

Section 5. **Date Effective**

Sections 1 and 2 shall take effect on the fifteenth day of October following the ratification of this article.

Section 6. **Limited Time for Ratification**

This article shall be inoperative unless it shall have been ratified as an amendment to the Constitution by the legislatures of three-fourths of the several States within seven years from the date of its submission.

Amendment 21
(Ratified in 1933, after 9½ months)

REPEAL OF THE PROHIBITION AMENDMENT

Section 1. **Repeal of Amendment 18**

The eighteenth article of amendment to the Constitution of the United States is hereby repealed.

Section 2. **States Protected**

The transportation or importation into any State, territory or possession of the United States for delivery or use therein of intoxicating liquors in violation of the laws thereof, is hereby prohibited.

Section 3. **Limited Time for Ratification**

This article shall be inoperative unless it shall have been ratified as an amendment to the Constitution by conventions in the several States, as provided in the Constitution, within seven years from the date of the submission hereof to the States by the Congress.

It was ratified within a year by all 48 states.

Repealing the 18th Amendment, the 21st is the only one to be ratified by states' conventions rather than by states' legislatures. (North Carolina chose not to hold a convention.)

A promise of Federal help for enforcement of Prohibition laws in the dry states. (Some counties, but no states, are still dry.)

The 13th and the 21st are the only Amendments that can be directly violated by individuals.

Franklin D. Roosevelt was and will be the only President ever elected to a third—and to a fourth!—term. Republicans, incensed at F.D.R.'s repeated Democratic successes, pressed for restricted Presidential tenure. The 22nd Amendment took the longest to be ratified—almost four years. It is the only Amendment to be secured by conservative political forces. Jefferson did not like the idea that a President could succeed himself, but he succeeded himself in the 1804 election—the only Vice President also to serve two full terms as President.

Amendment 22
(Ratified in 1951, after 3 years, 11½ months)

TWO-TERM AMENDMENT

Section 1. **Presidential Term Limited**

No person shall be elected to the office of the President more than twice, and no person who has held the office of President, or acted as President, for more than two years of a term to which some other person was elected President shall be elected to the office of the President more than once. But this article shall not apply to any person holding the office of President when this article was proposed by the Congress, and shall not prevent any person who may be holding the office of President, or acting as President, during the term within which this article becomes operative from holding the office of President or acting as President during the remainder of such term.

Section 2. **Limited Time for Ratification**

This article shall be inoperative unless it shall have been ratified as an amendment to the Constitution by the legislatures of three-fourths of the several States within seven years from the date of its submission to the States by the Congress.

Amendment 23
(Ratified in 1961, after 9 months)

WASHINGTON, D.C., VOTE

Section 1. **Appointment of Electors**

The District constituting the seat of Government of the United States shall appoint in such manner as the Congress may direct: A number of electors of President and Vice President equal to the whole number of Senators and Representatives in Congress to which the District would be entitled if it were a State, but in no event more than the least populous State; they shall be in addition to those appointed by the States, but they shall be considered, for the purposes of the election of President and Vice President, to be electors appointed by a State; and they shall meet in the District and perform such duties as provided by the twelfth article of amendment.

Section 2. **Enforcement**

The Congress shall have power to enforce this article by appropriate legislation.

Eleven Presidents have been defeated in their re-election bids by the voters or by their own political parties.

At the convention, Richard Bassett, a Delaware delegate, was the first to vote for relocating the U.S. capital to an independent Federal enclave on

the banks of the Potomac River. Ten weeks after the Congress of the Confederation had transacted its last official business (October 10, 1788), Maryland ceded 10 square miles to Congress for a Federal city. President Washington himself picked the exact site for the capitol, at the geographic midpoint between Northern financiers and Southern farmers. The nation's capital was in New York through 1790, then in Philadelphia until the District of Columbia (pop. 14,000) was ready for operation, in 1800. D.C.'s population doubled during the War Between the States, when thousands of freed black slaves sought a haven there. Plans are afoot to make the District of Columbia a full-fledged state.

Five Amendments—12, 20, 22, 23, and 25—concern the executive branch of the Federal government.

Amendment 24
(Ratified in 1964, after 1 year, 5½ months)

ABOLITION OF POLL TAXES

Section 1. Voting Rights

The right of citizens of the United States to vote in any primary or other election for President or Vice President, for electors for President or Vice President, or for Senator or Representative in Congress, shall not be denied or abridged by the United States or any State by reason of failure to pay any poll tax or other tax.

Section 2. Enforcement

The Congress shall have power to enforce this article by appropriate legislation.

Amendment 25
(Ratified in 1967, after 1 year, 6½ months)

PRESIDENTIAL SUCCESSION

Section 1. Vice President Becomes President

In case of the removal of the President from office or of his death or resignation, the Vice President shall become President.

Section 2. Filling the Vice Presidency

Whenever there is a vacancy in the office of the Vice President, the President shall nominate a Vice President who shall take office upon confirmation by a majority vote of both houses of Congress.

Section 3. Vice President as Acting President

Whenever the President transmits to the President pro tempore of the Senate and the Speaker of the House of Representatives his written declaration that he is unable to discharge the powers and duties of his office, and until he transmits to them a written declaration to the contrary, such powers and duties shall be discharged by the Vice President as Acting President.

Only five states still had the tax requirement: Alabama, Arkansas, Mississippi, Texas, and Virginia.

Nine Vice Presidents have succeeded to the Presidency.

The office of Vice President has been vacant 16 times, for a total of 37 years. Both of James Madison's Vice Presidents, George Clinton and Elbridge Gerry, died in office. (The Massachusetts delegate to the convention gave his name to the language: gerrymander.) The issue of Presidential succession and the plugging of the Vice Presidency was rekindled when President John F. Kennedy was slain in Dallas, in 1963. (Eight Presidents have died in office.)

The 25th Amendment was invoked in 1973 when Spiro Agnew became the second Vice President to quit the office. (John C. Calhoun, one of two Vice Presidents to serve two different Presidents, believed he could better represent his native South Carolina as a Senator.) Agnew, in trouble with the law for kickbacks as Maryland Governor, was succeeded by Congressman Gerald R. Ford, who had never faced a national election. Less than a year later, President Richard M. Nixon quit under fire and Ford became President; Nelson A. Rockefeller became Ford's Vice President—the only one ever to be appointed. Ford was defeated when he ran against Jimmy Carter, in 1976.

Section 4. **Presidential Incapacity**

Whenever the Vice President and a majority of either the principal officers of the executive departments or of such other body as Congress may by law provide, transmit to the President pro tempore of the Senate and the Speaker of the House of Representatives their written declaration that the President is unable to discharge the powers and duties of his office, the Vice President shall immediately assume the powers and duties of the office as Acting President.

President resumes office. Thereafter, when the President transmits to the President pro tempore of the Senate and the Speaker of the House of Representatives his written declaration that no inability exists, he shall resume the powers and duties of his office unless the Vice President and a majority of either the principal officers of the executive department or of such other body as Congress may by law provide, transmit within four days to the President pro tempore of the Senate and the Speaker of the House of Representatives their written declaration that the President is unable to discharge the powers and duties of his office. Thereupon Congress shall decide the issue, assembling within forty-eight hours for that purpose if not in session. If the Congress, within twenty-one days after receipt of the latter written declaration, or, if Congress is not in session, within twenty-one days after Congress is required to assemble, determines by two-thirds vote of both houses that the President is unable to discharge the powers and duties of his office, the Vice President shall continue to discharge the same as Acting President; otherwise, the President shall resume the powers and duties of his office.

Amendment 26

(Ratified in 1971, after 4 months)

EXTENDING THE VOTE TO EIGHTEEN YEAR OLDS

Section 1. **Eighteen-Year-Old Suffrage**

The right of citizens of the United States, who are eighteen years of age or older, to vote shall not be denied or abridged by the United States or by any State on account of age.

Section 2. **Enforcement**

The Congress shall have power to enforce this article by appropriate legislation.

Four states had already let under-21s vote: Hawaii, 20; Alaska, 19; Kentucky and Georgia, 18.

Three of the last five Amendments have extended the franchise (as would have the Equal Rights Amendment).

By the process of amendment and construction, the Constitution has been found adaptable to the solution of a steady succession of problems affecting our national life. Former Chief Justice Warren Burger says a second convention for review of the Constitution would be a "giant waste of time." But there are statesmen and scholars who believe the unique "separation of powers" leads to debilitating conflict, stalemate, and deadlock.

In 1814, the original four-page Constitution was moved from the nation's capital to Leesburg, Va., before the imminent attack on Washington by the British. (President James Madison fled before Redcoats put the torch to the city.) Later, it was hidden away from public view, folded up in a little tin box in the lower part of a closet in the State Department. In 1921, President Warren G. Harding ordered it displayed. During the Second World War, the Constitution was sheltered in Fort Knox, Ky. On December 13, 1952, the Constitution and the Declaration of Independence were placed in helium-filled cases enclosed in wooden crates that were laid on mattresses in an armored Marine Corps personnel carrier. Escorted by ceremonial troops, two tanks, and four servicemen carrying submachine guns, the documents were moved from the Library of Congress and installed in the National Archives, where they reside today. (The middle pages of the Constitution are kept in a vault and displayed only on Constitution Day, September 17.)

Amendment 27
(Ratified in 1992, after 202 years, 8 months)

COMPENSATION TO MEMBERS OF CONGRESS

No law, varying the compensation for the services of the Senators and Representatives, shall take effect, until an election of Representatives shall have intervened.

The Constitution passed its greatest test in the 1860s, when the Civil War once and for all settled the questions of a strong Union and centralized, strengthened Federal power. The War, from one perspective, was the submission of incompatible interpretations of the Constitution to the arbitrament of arms.

The American Historical Association and the American Political Science Association (Project '87) vouchsafe there are today 13 enduring constitutional issues:

National Power: limits and potential. *Federalism:* the balance between nation and state. *The Judiciary:* interpreter of the Constitution or shaper of public policy. *Civil Liberties:* the balance between government and the individual. *Criminal Penalties:* rights of the accused and protection of the community. *Equality:* its definition as a constitutional value. *The Rights of Women Under the Constitution. The Rights of Ethnic and Racial Groups Under the Constitution. Presidential Power in Wartime and in Foreign Affairs. The Separation of Powers and the Capacity to Govern. Avenues of Representation. Property Rights and Economic Policy. Constitutional Change and Flexibility.*

Thomas Jefferson, who believed "laws and institutions must go hand in hand with the progress of the human mind," once wrote, "The tree of liberty must be refreshed from time to time with the blood of its patriots and tyrants. It is its natural manure."